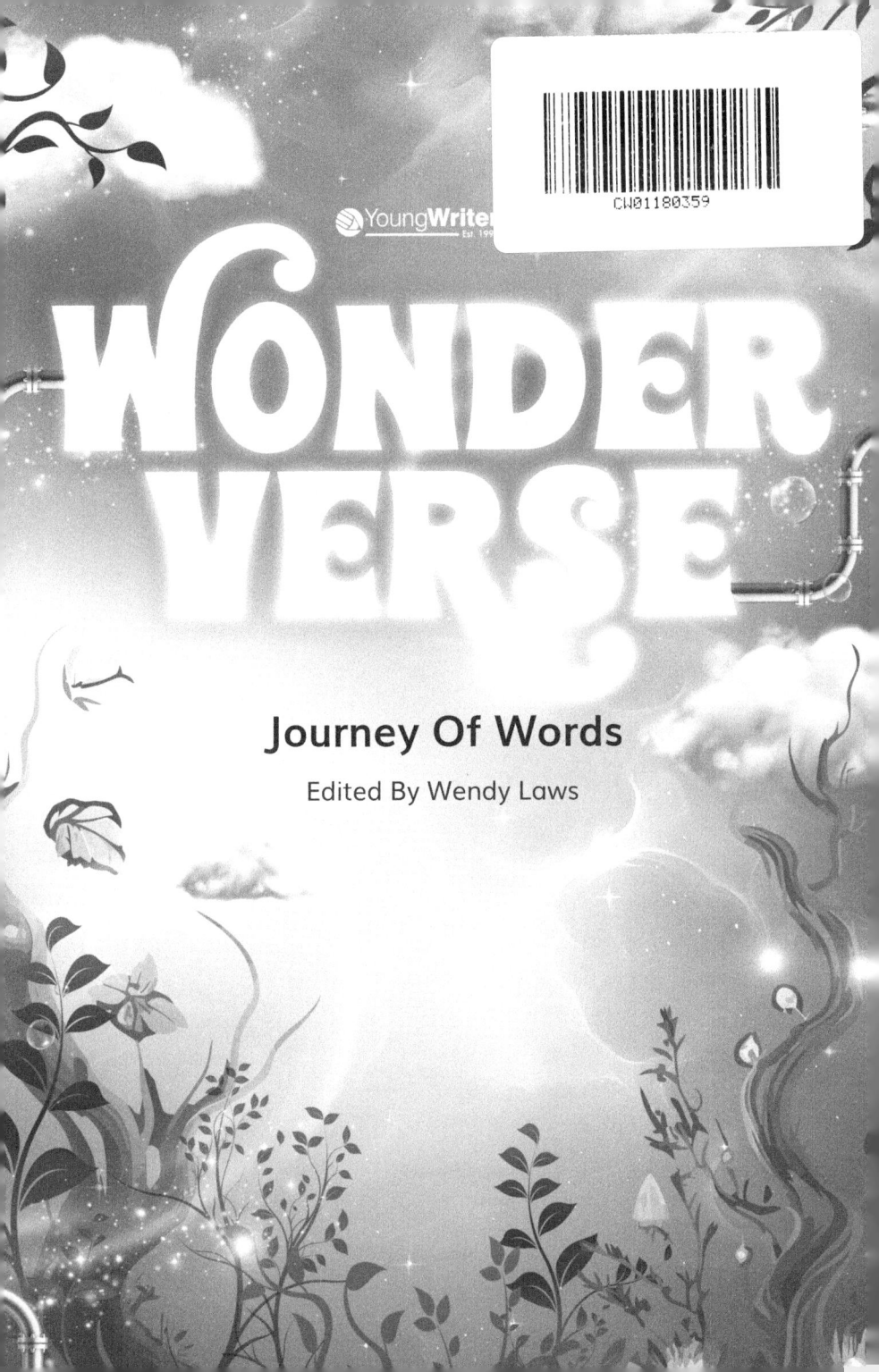

WONDER VERSE

Journey Of Words

Edited By Wendy Laws

First published in Great Britain in 2024 by:

Young Writers
Est. 1991

Young Writers
Remus House
Coltsfoot Drive
Peterborough
PE2 9BF
Telephone: 01733 890066
Website: www.youngwriters.co.uk

All Rights Reserved
Book Design by Davina Hopping
© Copyright Contributors 2024
Softback ISBN 978-1-83685-062-5
Printed and bound in the UK by BookPrintingUK
Website: www.bookprintinguk.com
YB0620G

FOREWORD

Welcome Reader,

For Young Writers' latest competition *Wonderverse*, we asked primary school pupils to explore their creativity and write a poem on any topic that inspired them. They rose to the challenge magnificently with some going even further and writing stories too! The result is this fantastic collection of writing in a variety of styles.

Here at Young Writers our aim is to encourage creativity in children and to inspire a love of the written word, so it's great to get such an amazing response, with some absolutely fantastic pieces. This open theme of this competition allowed them to write freely about something they are interested in, which we know helps to engage kids and get them writing. Within these pages you'll find a variety of topics, from hopes, fears and dreams, to favourite things and worlds of imagination. The result is a collection of brilliant writing that showcases the creativity and writing ability of the next generation.

I'd like to congratulate all the young writers in this anthology, I hope this inspires them to continue with their creative writing.

CONTENTS

Aberdour Primary School, Aberdour

Lucy Salmon	1
Millie Stewart (9)	2
Connor Cook (8)	3
Harriet Smillie Gray (9)	4
Miller Irvine (8)	5
Ilisa Molloy	6
Ellie Shankland	7
Cameron Dillon (9)	8
Charlie Dawson (9)	9
Amalie Macfarlane (8)	10
Eva McLachlan (9)	11
Ava Cook (9)	12
Nairn Davidson	13
Edith Toddie-Moore (9)	14
Robin Stockwell (8)	15
Jocelyn Sweeney	16
Erla Johnson (9)	17
Otto Trouw	18
Hannah Kyle (8)	19
Mhairi Brand (9)	20
Leon Munn-Ritchie	21

Colinsburgh Primary School, Colinsburgh

Oona Minick (10)	22
Eva Montgomery (11)	23
Bonnie Ednie (8)	24
Charlotte Zielinski (10)	25
Cameron Kippen (11)	26
Emma Stuart (9)	27
Alex Pryde (11)	28
Nea Grace Heikal-Shackelford (9)	29

Jack O'Reilly (9)	30
Rachel McGowan (10)	31
Beth Hobday (11)	32
Elina Creevy (9)	33
Ross Laurie (10)	34
Lucy Kippen (9)	35

Donibristle Primary School, Dalgety Bay

Bridgette Bojdo-Campbell (9)	36
Ava White (9)	37
Lydia MacKean (9)	38
Eilidh Rafferty (8)	39
Poppy Murray (9)	40
Camilia Thabet (9)	41
Ada Grayland (8)	42
Lucia Rose Payne (9)	43
Zoey Dewar (9)	44
Autumn Allan (9)	45
Iona Dewar (9)	46
Jessica Needham (9)	47
Cara Cochrane (9)	48
Sacha Hutt (9)	49
Grace Fraser (9)	50
Niven Semple (9)	51
William Routledge (9)	52
Elinor Flint (9)	53
Mya Henderson (9)	54
Sophie Harvey (9)	55
Robin McDonald (9)	56
Ethan Oliver (9)	57
Sophia Di Carlo (9)	58

Newark Hill Academy, Peterborough

Agnes Mason (8)	59
Raiyaan Abdul (8)	60
Samanta Grinvalde (8)	61
Tallulla Prudames (8)	62
Emilis Valciukas (8)	63
Anna Cham (8)	64
Casey Marr (8)	65
Moeez (9)	66
Ellis Michael Do Carmo (9)	67
Amaya Khan (8)	68
Oliver Cavender (8)	69
Jessica Branscombe (8)	70
Lauren Catinean (8)	71
Allan Benjamin Calocane (8)	72
Nicole Kukolik (8)	73
Zara Rasool (8)	74
Faisal Amarkhil (8)	75
Daniel Nourozi (8)	76
Fatima Faisal (8)	77
Zainab Rafiq (8)	78
Joshua (8)	79
Inaaya Ahmed (8)	80
Khadijah Choudhury (8)	81
Sapphire Harrison (8)	82
Natas Maksimavicius (9)	83
Shia Mackereth Lopes (8)	84
Evan Puckys (8)	85

Sutton Oak CE Primary School, St Helens

Ezekiel Oyemakinde (9)	86
Liana Mohammed (9)	87
Emmanuel Olaojoyetan (9)	88
Harry Carruthers (9)	89
Lucia Graham (9)	90
Jayden Lawrence (9)	91
Noah Gittins (9)	92
Ianna Boslan (9)	93
Leighton Bamber (9)	94
Amelia Willis (10)	95
Charlie Jones (9)	96
Logan Pickering (10)	97
Isobel Crawley (10)	98
Freddie Norton (9)	99

The Meadows Primary Academy, Blurton

Joe Williams (11)	100
Muhaiminul Karim Arish (10)	101
Annabelle Doyle (9)	102
Ryder Smithson (8)	103
Jaydah Carter	104
Erin Underwood (10)	105
Phoebe Ann Coglon (9)	106
Harper Lear (9)	107
Lewis Harvey (9)	108
Daniel Mair (9)	109
James Day (8)	110
Amber Jones (9)	111
Jovi Ray Smith (9)	112
Miley Pattinson (8)	113
Maddie Lamb (8)	114
George Mills (8)	115
Layla Edwards (8)	116
Taylor-Bow Higginson (10)	117
Nicole Norcup (9)	118
Benjamin Harrison (9)	119
Kaylee-Rae Gordon (10)	120
Aubry-Lea Sketchley (9)	121
Phoebe Green (8)	122
Isabelle Burgess-Lowe (9)	123
Mya Davies (7)	124
Thomas Hackney (11)	125
Kye Comley (10)	126
Cameron Bowman (8)	127
Adrian Majkowski (8)	128
Joseph Harrington (10)	129
Charlie Cotterill (10)	130
Isaac Mellor (7)	131
Lara Rauf (10)	132
Evelyn Pattinson (8)	133
Yusuf Aiybokhaodu	134
Davi Silveira Cozzo Tajariol (8)	135

Name	Page
Isla Cooper (8)	136
Jagoda (7)	137
Vincent Ehimen (10)	138
Evan Robotham (10)	139
Edom Aregay (9)	140
Imogen Speake (9)	141
Aimee Flynn (10)	142
Samuel Cragg (7)	143
Lottie Colclough (10)	144
Caleb Almarales (10)	145
Amber Clowes (10)	146
Shahzaib Akhtar (8)	147
Harlow Gollins (9)	148
Harley Lear (10)	149
Ivy Turner (8)	150
Lola Wakelin (10)	151
Evie Salmon (9)	152
Lily Sutton (10)	153
Olivia-Rae Nicklin (10)	154
Cody Prince (10)	155
Eleesie Lily Thorley	156
Tilly-Mae Podmore (7)	157
Jacob Dillon (10)	158
Harley Carr (8)	159
Reggie Rowland (7)	160
Noah Lovatt (11)	161
Tia Shey (9)	162
Isabelle Moran-Bamford (9)	163
Noah Smith-Harrison (9)	164
Lyla Ridge (10)	165
Callum Ford (10)	166
Ivy Clarke (10)	167
Thomas Fairbanks (9)	168
Tia Hilton (10)	169
Ibrahim Mahammad (8)	170
Destiny Babic (9)	171
Amadou Mbengue (8)	172
Isla-Rose Summerhayes (10)	173
Freddie Cragg (9)	174
Michael Giblin (10)	175
Amelia Allt (9)	176
Sebastian Mellor (9)	177
Eivelyn Baldwin (8)	178
Daisy Preston (9)	179
Harrison Crayton (7)	180
Charlie Kean (9)	181
Ezaan Raza (9)	182
Ryley Seadon (9)	183
Jessica Cliffe (7)	184
Ralph Clarke (8)	185
Peyton Harnett (8)	186
Dacey Jones (9)	187
Klayton Mellor (10) & Jessica Ann Pass (9)	188
Lexie Concliffe (10)	189
Oscar Edge (8)	190
Ava Emami (8)	191
Emil Joby (9)	192
Jack Sellers (9)	193
Gracie Oates (9)	194
Muhammad Narooz (9)	195
Penelope Woodall (10)	196
Eliza-Rae Steveson (10)	197
Marnie Cartlidge (8)	198
Freddie Hughes (8)	199
Harrison Crayton (7)	200
Eden Rose (8)	201
Aylan Rhys Lapi (8)	202
Jessica Gilham (7)	203
Harper Howell (9)	204
Freddie Ridge (7)	205
Joshua Millard (8)	206
Ada Watts (8)	207
John Osei (10)	208
Sharon Gwandu (9)	209
Oliver Loftus (7)	210
Dominik Olah (7)	211
Aronas Avdulovas (8)	212
Ideraoluwa Aliu (10)	213
Charlotte White (7)	214
Siena Cooper (11)	215
Ethan Cope (8)	216
Charlotte Dawson (8)	217
Nyla Bosha (11)	218
Wilfred Lees (7)	219
Alan Joby (7)	220

Victoria Ptak (8)	221
Avia Helliwell (7)	222
Olivia Coglon	223
Roman Adams (7)	224
Safoorah Malik (9)	225
Harley Brian (10)	226
Maximilian Almarales (8)	227
Ellie Cole-Pye (7)	228
Emma Jandzikova (8)	229
Isaac Nicklin (7)	230
Charlee-May O'Brien (7)	231

THE CREATIVE WRITING

Night Animals

Trying to survive.
Hunting for tasty meals now.
The moonlight shines down on us.
Wolves howling at the full moon.
Animals living their lives.

Lucy Salmon
Aberdour Primary School, Aberdour

Autumn

A tanka

Autumn is here now.
Having fun in the leaves now.
Hot chocolate's warm.
Leaves say goodbye to the trees.
The leaves are colours of fire.

Millie Stewart (9)
Aberdour Primary School, Aberdour

Frogs

A tanka

Frogs jump very high.
They leap across lily pads.
Sticking their tongues out.
Flies are super scared of them.
I think they are pretty cool.

Connor Cook (8)
Aberdour Primary School, Aberdour

Spring

A tanka

Spring is wonderful.
The leaves are blooming fast now.
People do love spring.
The days are nice and warmer.
People swimming in the sea.

Harriet Smillie Gray (9)
Aberdour Primary School, Aberdour

Football

A tanka

A football is fun.
Kick it all around the pitch.
It is dangerous.
It is both crazy and fun.
Take shots, score goals. It's all fun.

Miller Irvine (8)
Aberdour Primary School, Aberdour

I Love Food

A tanka

Like a fluffy cloud,
Mashed potato in my mouth
With silk gravy now.
Let's have dessert so tasty.
Ice cream with raspberries now.

Ilisa Molloy
Aberdour Primary School, Aberdour

The Jungle

A tanka

Monkeys climbing trees.
Snakes slithering sneakily.
Frogs jumping up high.
Parrots flying very high.
Hedgehogs walking very cute.

Ellie Shankland
Aberdour Primary School, Aberdour

Pigs
A tanka

A mini best friend,
Very cute rolling in mud,
Pigs rule the mammals.
Really cute pigs eating fruit,
A lovely friend to play with.

Cameron Dillon (9)
Aberdour Primary School, Aberdour

Animals

A tanka

Chickens laying eggs.
Big orange tigers lurking
Around the jungle.
Monkeys swinging from big trees,
The others are eating fruit.

Charlie Dawson (9)
Aberdour Primary School, Aberdour

My Pet Cat

A tanka

He is amazing,
The best cat in the whole world,
He is fun and kind.
My whole beautiful wide world,
He is the most fun for me!

Amalie Macfarlane (8)
Aberdour Primary School, Aberdour

Summer

A tanka

The sun is beaming.
The sun is bright like a light.
Beautiful hotness.
The sun is blazing hot now.
The golden sun is today.

Eva McLachlan (9)
Aberdour Primary School, Aberdour

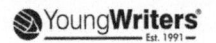

Dogs

A tanka

The very best pet.
A cute fluffy ball of joy
Super wonderful.
They make me feel so happy
And warm. I love dogs too much.

Ava Cook (9)
Aberdour Primary School, Aberdour

The Dog

He plays and jumps.
He is a cute ball of energy.
He is really fast.
Extraordinary dog.
Cute ball of fluff and energy.

Nairn Davidson
Aberdour Primary School, Aberdour

Summer

A tanka

Summer is so hot
The sea is as cold as ice.
The sun in my eyes.
Having a super ice cream.
Going swimming in the sea.

Edith Toddie-Moore (9)
Aberdour Primary School, Aberdour

Autumn

A tanka

Cool breezes around.
Animals hibernating.
I feel so cosy.
Leaves falling like waterfalls.
A big blanket of colour.

Robin Stockwell (8)
Aberdour Primary School, Aberdour

My Puppy

They are cosy and
So very adorable.
So much love around.
A big ball of fluff and joy.
I love my puppy so much!

Jocelyn Sweeney
Aberdour Primary School, Aberdour

My Cat, Patsy

Little ninja cat.
A cute ball of laziness.
Amazingly exotic.
Sneaky, soft, adorable,
Exciting, fantastic cat!

Erla Johnson (9)
Aberdour Primary School, Aberdour

Cats

A tanka

Cuddly and so soft.
A cute ball of energy.
Perfecting their fur.
Reflexes like a lion.
Energy like a cheetah.

Otto Trouw
Aberdour Primary School, Aberdour

Puppy

A cute ball of fluff.
So very adorable.
Cute as a button.
Such a playful pup.
I love my puppy so much!

Hannah Kyle (8)
Aberdour Primary School, Aberdour

Aberdour, My Home

A tanka

A doll's house village.
A majority of fun!
A train station and
A clock and telephone box.
A festival of fun here!

Mhairi Brand (9)
Aberdour Primary School, Aberdour

Cats

A haiku

Play with wool and string.
As sneaky as a ninja.
Furry cats walking.

Leon Munn-Ritchie
Aberdour Primary School, Aberdour

Fairy Forest

In the fairy forest, everything is quiet,
There is never any fuss, there's never any riot.
In the fairy forest, all the seasons change.
In total there are four seasons, that's a very wide range.
The fairy forest has fairies of course,
But outside, there is a very strong force.
The force is so strong,
You can't even hear their fairy forest song.
It turns out they've been here all along.
In the fairy forest there is a special tree,
It is so special the human eye can't see.
The tree is split up into four,
In the middle, there is a door.
Go inside, see what you can see,
There are four islands in a rainbow sea.
The four islands are all the seasons.
They are there for all the right reasons.
They are there to keep them safe,
To keep the seasons at the right place.

Oona Minick (10)
Colinsburgh Primary School, Colinsburgh

The Magical Village

There was once a girl named Eve.
She lived in a magical village
With a wee woodland at the side of their home.
Eve liked to go on little walks at night.
This was a new home for Eve and her family
So Eve decided to go for a little walk.
The branches crunched beneath her feet
Like crunching snow on frosty mornings.
Two hours into Eve's walk...
Boom, crack!
Eve heard a sound.
She shouted, "Who's there?"
Two girls popped out of a bush.
"Hi, I'm Charlotte."
"Hi, I'm Emma."
They met at a magical castle.

Eva Montgomery (11)
Colinsburgh Primary School, Colinsburgh

Friendship Never Ends

Ella's BFF and Zoe were planning to go on a hike,
The next day, Zoe and Ella packed their bags,
They went on the hike.
"Hi Ella," said Zoe.
"Yes," said Ella.
"Well..."
Zoe was scared to tell her.
"What?" said Ella.
"Well... a... storm is coming," Zoe said.
Ella got scared!
"Well... let's get our minds off of it."
"Like... with what?"
"Well... look at the violets, at the red rose...
Please get your mind off the storm."
"Okay."

Bonnie Ednie (8)
Colinsburgh Primary School, Colinsburgh

Butterflies

B utterflies and birds fly above the sea
U nder the sea, creatures flow about the place
T he birds are tweeting
T here are lots of jellyfish in the sea
E very sea creature
R ing bubbles are made
F ish are swimming away from sharks
L ovely dolphins are diving in and out of the water
I sabella is the name of the whale
E lla and Eva are the butterflies' names
S tella is the butterflies' BFF!

Charlotte Zielinski (10)
Colinsburgh Primary School, Colinsburgh

Space

I see black skies where the moon lies.
Empty wonders where dreams are made.
Comets swooshing past me.
I hear nothing, it's as quiet as night.
I touch the zero gravity air on my flight through space.
I smell moon rocks when I land with advanced settings.
I don't need a spacesuit.
I'm drifting.
I taste the bitter space air as I'm drifting.
Moon rock crunching under my feet.
I wonder how long I'm staying.

Cameron Kippen (11)
Colinsburgh Primary School, Colinsburgh

Friendship

F riends are fun to play with
R eal friendship is going to stay together
I t is fun to play hide-and-seek
E mma is friends with Nea and Lucy
N ever fight together
D ance is what we like to do
S ea is nice and calm
H ouses up high but we play down below
I ncredible people are friends together
P lease, can we be friends forever in our life?

Emma Stuart (9)
Colinsburgh Primary School, Colinsburgh

Space Dog

S tar chaser
P lanet jumper
A steroid catcher
C osmic star
E arthling

D igger of the black holes
O n a rocket
G reat dog.

Alex Pryde (11)
Colinsburgh Primary School, Colinsburgh

Family

F amily is fun
A family loves their child or children
M ums and dads be strong
I love my family
L ittle ones make some fun
Y ummy food I get to eat!

Nea Grace Heikal-Shackelford (9)
Colinsburgh Primary School, Colinsburgh

Pikachu

P ikachu is my favourite
I love Pikachu's fluffy face!
K ing Pikachu
A mazing
C ute
H orrifyingly adorable!
U nderstands Ash!

Jack O'Reilly (9)
Colinsburgh Primary School, Colinsburgh

An Autumn Wood

Birds chirping
Leaves crunching
Branches waving
Conkers falling
Brambles growing
Rocks rolling
Trees swaying
People playing
Paths overgrown.

Rachel McGowan (10)
Colinsburgh Primary School, Colinsburgh

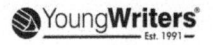

The Woods

Trees swaying
Birds playing
Foxes snuffling
Bushes rustling
Deer hiding
Squirrels finding
Leaves falling
People calling
The woods.

Beth Hobday (11)
Colinsburgh Primary School, Colinsburgh

Candle Cave

C ave light
A glow as sweet as sugar
N ice and beautiful
D elicate
L ight
E nthusiastic with light.

Elina Creevy (9)
Colinsburgh Primary School, Colinsburgh

Horrible War

Gunshots blaring
Rainbows dying
People fighting
Bombs dropping
Tanks firing
People screaming.

Ross Laurie (10)
Colinsburgh Primary School, Colinsburgh

The Dazzling Dog

D azzling
O utstanding
G lamorous
S tunning.

Lucy Kippen (9)
Colinsburgh Primary School, Colinsburgh

Me And My Rabbits

M e and my rabbits play and play and the rabbits squeak as they play
E motions are everywhere, especially in me and my rabbits' hearts

A ngry is an emotion that me and my rabbits carry, *stomp, stomp*, I can be just like my rabbits
N aughty is my rabbit, Poppy, she is so naughty
D on't eat in front of a rabbit, *crunch, crunch*, because they get jealous

M y rabbits glow when they are happy
Y elp for help sometimes so we keep them safe from magpies, *scratch, scratch*

R abbits are rabbits and they have habits
A t night they have a midnight talk, *chatter, chatter*
B ut you always have to feed them, *yum, yum*
B ut they are always eating food, *tum, tum*
I n the winter they love more food and water, *slurp, slurp*
T hey always hop lots of miles, *stomp, stomp*
S miles are a great feeling even when you have two fluff balls next to you to make you smile, *stroke, stroke.*

Bridgette Bojdo-Campbell (9)
Donibristle Primary School, Dalgety Bay

Save The Planet

P lanet Earth is our home
L ike the one you own
A little treat every day
N ear your house is a school
E ver have you thought to pick up mouldy wool?
T race and go to outer space and walk at a steady pace.

E veryone can make out of flowers a piece of art
A nd if you clean up Planet Earth then you will have a good laugh
R are things are everywhere on Earth
T here are loads of wonderful stuff in outer space, maybe a strawberry lace
H ave you ever been to outer space? If you have you walked at a steady pace.

Ava White (9)
Donibristle Primary School, Dalgety Bay

My Autumn Walk

M y favourite season to go for a walk is autumn
Y ou can look for conkers

A nd see all the colourful leaves
U p in the trees the leaves fall off to the ground
T o be picked up and made into art
U mbrellas bobbing along the pavements keeping everybody dry
M any people staying inside keeping warm
N ights getting darker and longer

W eather getting colder and windier
A nd so we wear cosy clothes
L ots of yummy treats to get at Halloween
K nowing winter is just around the corner.

Lydia MacKean (9)
Donibristle Primary School, Dalgety Bay

My Mummy Is Pregnant!

I have some news about my mummy,
She has a baby in her tummy.
Guess what?
It is a baby boy.
I am filled with so much joy.
I am so happy
But I don't want to change his stinky nappy.
What should we name him?
What about Jim?
I am so excited to teach him how to walk,
I'm sure it won't be long until he can talk.
He might be born in February or May,
Either way, I can't wait to play.
I am having a baby brother really soon!

Eilidh Rafferty (8)
Donibristle Primary School, Dalgety Bay

Save The Planet

I saved the planet. *Splish, splash, splish, splash.*
I did it as a plan. *Splish, splash, splish, splash.*
Tell me I did it. *Splish, splash, splish, splash.*
I was an astronaut. *Splish, splash, splish, splash.*
I was in front of a planet. *Splish, splash, splish, splash.*
Tell me I wasn't. *Splish, splash, splish, splash.*
I really was. *Splish, splash, splish, splash.*

Poppy Murray (9)
Donibristle Primary School, Dalgety Bay

About Me

C amilia is my name
A nd I've got no roaring lion's mane
M y favourite book is 'Harry Potter'
I like it somewhere a bit hotter
L ike everyone, I like a treat
I don't really like to dance to a beat
A nd lastly, Eleyna and Elinor are my friends.

Camilia Thabet (9)
Donibristle Primary School, Dalgety Bay

Spring Is Springing!

Spring is my favourite,
Birds cheeping in their nests,
New flowers in the garden,
The sun shining on the water,
BBQ sizzling for tea,
Burgers and hot dogs, yummy!
Spring is my favourite,
Lambs are jumping in the fields,
Flowers grow and trees bloom,
The snow goes away.
Hip hip hooray!

Ada Grayland (8)
Donibristle Primary School, Dalgety Bay

My Life

My name is Lucia-Rose
And I love to swim and pose,
I have two big sisters
And one little mister
Who has been naughty ever since he was born.

I am the middle kid who loves school,
Even though I hate all the rules,
My sisters have a rare condition
And it is my mission
To find a cure.

Lucia Rose Payne (9)
Donibristle Primary School, Dalgety Bay

Nature

N o litter should be seen
A mazing sights and views
T he animals go munch and the leaves go crunch
U nder the ground, animals stay nice and warm and are sleeping
R emember to put your litter in the bin
E veryone has to be kind to nature in hibernation season.

Zoey Dewar (9)
Donibristle Primary School, Dalgety Bay

Autumn - The Season

A utumn, my wonderful unique name
U nder the ground hedgehogs stay
T umble and turn in the crunching leaves
U nder the ground creepy-crawlies stay
M ud squishes under your feet
N umbers of creepy-crawlies are crawling for a treat!

I love autumn!

Autumn Allan (9)
Donibristle Primary School, Dalgety Bay

Nature

N atural environment is very good for nature
A ll are welcome to help nature
T rouble with nature means trouble with animals
U nderground hibernation happens after autumn
R emember to never litter, *crunch, crunch*
E veryone helps us.

Iona Dewar (9)
Donibristle Primary School, Dalgety Bay

Happy, Sad, Mad Young Space

Please don't be mad,
You can be a bit happy and sad,
I am really happy that you're with me.

Sad, mad, glad, bad, good lad,
Are you still sad?
Always you are mad and glad.

Hey, hey, yay,
Come and play today, please,
You're my favourite.

Jessica Needham (9)
Donibristle Primary School, Dalgety Bay

Nature

N o litter should be found
A nimals go munch with a crunch
T o be kind to nature
U nderground hibernation can take place in winter
R emember not to litter
E veryone has to treat nature kindly all year especially in hibernation season.

Cara Cochrane (9)
Donibristle Primary School, Dalgety Bay

Winter

W inter is frosty cold
I love to play in the very cold snow
N o one likes cold snow down their back
T eachers get the icy holidays off
E veryone loves a snowball
R unning in the snow is so much fun!

Sacha Hutt (9)
Donibristle Primary School, Dalgety Bay

Let's Be Off

F ierce dragons
R eindeer on the snow
I n crowds when playing
E lephants clump all over the ground
N ew unicorn friends
D ull, dark, lonely night
S unny days when you wake up.

Grace Fraser (9)
Donibristle Primary School, Dalgety Bay

Summer

S ummer is delicate
U p in a hot air balloon
M y ice cream is melting
M y bother is too, *drip, drip*
E verything is delicate in summer
R oad trip, we had a nice road trip!

Niven Semple (9)
Donibristle Primary School, Dalgety Bay

Autumn

Leaves go red, orange and gold.
I crunch through fallen leaves.
The smell of a bonfire in the distance.
Smoke curls up into the sky.
Conkers fall from their spiky shells
And leaves start to fall from the trees.

William Routledge (9)
Donibristle Primary School, Dalgety Bay

Emotions

E motions are like a hissing sea
L et them roam free
I nside you they lie
N ow let me tell you some to exemplify
O verjoyed to super annoyed
R oaring mad to really glad.

Elinor Flint (9)
Donibristle Primary School, Dalgety Bay

Happy

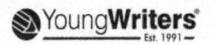

H appiness we all need
A great way to feel
P eople who are happy make your life so unsnappy
P ups have the same idea
Y ou've just got to smile.

Mya Henderson (9)
Donibristle Primary School, Dalgety Bay

My Piano Test

P lanning a test to win
I just have to put up my chin
A nd pack away my book
N otes crackled down the crook
O pen the piano to play, to look.

Sophie Harvey (9)
Donibristle Primary School, Dalgety Bay

Space

S pace is slow
P eace comes in a flow
A ll shooting stars have a glow
C ool is space, space is cool
E ternal darkness.

Robin McDonald (9)
Donibristle Primary School, Dalgety Bay

The Moon

M oons glow bright
O n a faraway planet
O n an amazing night
N ow I bet there's an alien called Hannet.

Ethan Oliver (9)
Donibristle Primary School, Dalgety Bay

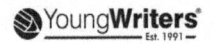

Nature

I saw a bunny hopping.
I saw a butterfly flying.
I heard a bird singing.
I smelt lovely flowers.
I felt the wind in my hair.

Sophia Di Carlo (9)
Donibristle Primary School, Dalgety Bay

The Secret Of Autumn

Autumn is cold with a breeze,
Orange, brown and scarlet
Pumpkin showing off his vibrant tangerine,
Hungry squirrels stealing fourteen.

Autumn is keeping the vibrant and blowing the dark,
Mushrooms big and tall, round and small
Inside the glory treasure is to behold,
A land of autumn goods that fall.

The autumn is like a deer trotting,
Click, clack, crunch!
Running through forests and deep piles of leaves with hedgehogs burrowing deep,
Nibbling a bunch of lunch.

The autumn leaves fly as the wind whistles,
The leaves fly in tangerine,
All crackly and crunchy!
And trees left with thirteen.

Agnes Mason (8)
Newark Hill Academy, Peterborough

Autumn Lion

The autumn is a lion,
He snatches and catches food.
He smashes and dashes,
He touches and scrunches leaves.
He roars and soars,
He catches leaves and hatches his babies.

Autumn lion

The autumn is a lion,
He eats and keeps berries.
He shares and glares at leaves,
He hunts for nuts.
He kills and chills,
He gets leaves and gets animal thieves.

Autumn lion

The autumn is a lion,
He finds diamonds, gems, emeralds, crystals and rubies.
He takes them in his secret base all the way to space,
He seeks and peeks to get somebody else expensive, cool treasure.

Raiyaan Abdul (8)
Newark Hill Academy, Peterborough

The Autumn

Autumn is cold,
Collecting terracotta pumpkins
And a snowball mushroom.

A queen of flowers
Leaves flowing around a princess
As red as a ruby

Autumn is a crack of the leaves,
Magpies stealing gold
Shining in the trees

A princess dancing
Birds tapping
Squirrels running around having fun.

Autumn mushrooms sitting on the olive grass
Scarlet, red and daisy white
Gazing in the sun.

The autumn wind likes to wave around the trees
Leaves twirling down from the sky
Landing on the grassy ground.

Samanta Grinvalde (8)
Newark Hill Academy, Peterborough

Autumn Squirrel

Autumn is a squirrel,
Cheekily leaping and gliding,
As it wags its tail, making a gush of wind,
He starts leaping and hiding.

Autumn is a collector,
He collects bronze, rubies and emeralds
Then he puts them up high
For everyone to say oh my!

Autumn is a baby,
Squealing with long, noisy and sad tears,
But sometimes giggling so bright,
And other times calm and humming.

Autumn is an acrobat,
That enjoys to prance and twirl
He jumps so high he knocks down the leaves
And adores to dance and swirl.

Tallulla Prudames (8)
Newark Hill Academy, Peterborough

The Autumn Melody

The jubilant autumn spirit brings memories of treasure,
The cheeping bird sings in the dawn,
While leaves clatter together,
In the fresh lawn.

The leaves are a stroller,
Bushy and dry,
They spring all around,
Like an army twirling everywhere.

The cheeky children play,
The jubilant leaves flying with the wind,
Giggling, jumping,
Enjoying the view.

The leaves twist and twirl,
Building the clattering melody,
In the air,
Chatting and rattling everywhere.

Emilis Valciukas (8)
Newark Hill Academy, Peterborough

Autumn Fairy

Autumn is a magical fairy
The sun shines down on the orange, yellow and red leaves.
As the wind calmly glides
The leaves gently slide off the tree,
As the leaves fall, they start to dry up in the sun.
When the beautiful humans walk on the leaves, they crunch like munching on an apple.

The fire crackling in my soul makes me feel happy.
The fire is red like ruby with diamonds.
The leaves are twirling through the autumn forest.
The autumn cries with rain and sadness.

Anna Cham (8)
Newark Hill Academy, Peterborough

Autumn Is Here

She dances calmly in the wind with leaves waving, and leaves and berries falling off trees.

She collects conkers, leaves, and berries.
She is getting diamonds, and rain is like treasure.

She is singing softly like a bird and she dances and prances,
She spins, swirls, and whirls.

Throwing the leaves in the air,
Painting with wind, cold breeze, and leaves waving and with bright colours.
The autumn queen has powers,
Flick! And the thunder comes!

Casey Marr (8)
Newark Hill Academy, Peterborough

Autumn

Autumn is frosty,
Autumn is when the farmers gather
Crops, carrots, potatoes,
The autumn leaves fly.

Kids gather leaves and jump in,
They gather conkers
Off a conker tree.

Autumn is a bandit,
Stealing leaves,
Keeping leaves,
Throwing pebbles away.

The autumn is a lamb,
He giggles,
A leaf,
A spectacular leaf.

Autumn is a bandit,
As he rapidly bends,
Rushing in the streets,
A serenade, a dance.

Moeez (9)
Newark Hill Academy, Peterborough

Autumn King

He transforms the crunchy leaves into beautiful chestnut leaves.
He turns the trees into beautiful oak trees in pumpkin colour.
He can hear delightful chestnut leaves as he steps into the autumn leaves.
As he walks through the autumn leaves, he feels a beautiful bird feed on his feet.
He can see the beautiful chestnut leaves falling through the air, onto the ground
As the leaves fall onto the ground.
He can smell the chestnut leaves in the air, gliding through the air.

Ellis Michael Do Carmo (9)
Newark Hill Academy, Peterborough

The Autumn's Treasure

The autumn's a flower,
A blower, a wonder,
Pushing leaves out of the way,
As squirrels tuck under,

The autumn's a majesty,
A royal, a loyal,
Hunting for precious jewels
Under maroon and green leaves,

The autumn's a child,
A twirler, a whirler,
Flowing around with joy,
As it whirls around,

The autumn's a prancer,
A dancer, a ballerina,
Twirling and flowing,
Like a pirouette in an arena.

Amaya Khan (8)
Newark Hill Academy, Peterborough

Autumn

Autumn is a bandit,
Taking the leaf in the wind,
Autumn is playful,
Swirling as it grinned.

The autumn is hot,
Autumn is cold,
You better wear,
What you were told!

Autumn is a flower of leaves,
For kids to jump on,
Playing with a crunchy leaf,
Soon, it will all be gone.

Autumn is kind, young and an angel,
The swishy berries are yummy,
Autumn is yellow, red and orange,
Colourful flavours in my tummy.

Oliver Cavender (8)
Newark Hill Academy, Peterborough

Autumn Queen

Autumn is a queen, she floats around, gently pulling off the leaves.
Autumn twirls the leaves in the wind and under them are hazelnut conkers.
Autumn paints with squished berries, ruby and amethyst, blueberries
And all of the nice colours.
She squished berries to make paint
And painted the leaves with it.
Autumn dances and prances all around, gliding across the floor.
She twirls and swirls.
Autumn giggles as she watches the leaves blowing and flowing.

Jessica Branscombe (8)
Newark Hill Academy, Peterborough

Autumn Is A Wanderer

Autumn is a wanderer,
Walking as the leaves spin in the breeze,
Colourful leaves falling off trees,
Be careful not to sneeze.

Autumn's royalty,
A loyal queen,
Gathering emerald-green leaves,
As a daily routine.

Autumn's a child,
A joyful soul,
Falling in leaves,
Laughter getting out of control.

Autumn's a dancer,
A twirler, a spinner,
Tumbling to the groove,
A wonderful winner.

Lauren Catinean (8)
Newark Hill Academy, Peterborough

Autumn Prince

Autumn is a prince,
He plays games, goes outside,
Leaves crunch, gliding, rustling, and wind howling.
Acorns falling and pumpkin kisses and harvest wishes.
Happy pumpkin spice, look, it spins more.
He munches pumpkins, and birds are tweeting, he slobbers down shells and dews down the hill.
Autumn rain drowns, he gives emerald and diamonds.
Autumn is a collector,
He goes and gets diamonds cosy and jumps on half of the chestnut tree.

Allan Benjamin Calocane (8)
Newark Hill Academy, Peterborough

The Beauty Of Autumn

Autumn is cold,
Swirling the leaves to thunder,
The storm makes it jubilant,
Squirrels collecting acorns, precious jewels.

The breeze is cold,
It's wonderful how the leaves flow down,
Pumpkins and mushrooms grow tall,
It's shivering bright and colourful.

Autumn's a princess,
A colourful, leafy, swaying dress,
Hair creamy, waving in the wind,
Sitting in the beautiful autumn sunset.

Nicole Kukolik (8)
Newark Hill Academy, Peterborough

Autumn Evil Villain

She is heavily breathing, stomping on the falling leaves.
Looking at the fire with a burning picture, her voice roaring with a dash, hiding in a stash.

Her stealing is smooth like butter, stomping on leaves like their sleeves.
Sliding pearls in her hand.
Grabbing gems and sticking them under her body.

Screaming in the rain, depressed.
Being the bad blood she is, making trees cry.
She no longer has a heart.

Zara Rasool (8)
Newark Hill Academy, Peterborough

King Autumn

King Autumn dropping crunchy leaves from the chestnut trees.
Pumpkin plants, harvest pumpkin, yummy just to eat.
Autumn coughs making lots of fog.
Firewood crackling, burning hot, smoking in autumn.
King Autumn making hot chocolate with cocoa bean.
Sleeping in his cosy bed, in the night of Halloween.
Squirrels jumping tree to tree, eating nuts.
Trees losing leaves, getting cold.
Weather turning cold, frozen plants.

Faisal Amarkhil (8)
Newark Hill Academy, Peterborough

Autumn Queen

Autumn is a queen,
Birds are her miners,
They bring her berries,
They are the best finders.

Autumn is cool,
She makes animals come out,
She makes pumpkins,
And she paints the leaves.

Autumn blows wind,
She loves to do it,
You can feel it,
But you can't see it.

Autumn is a performer,
She sings lullabies to the hedgehogs,
And she dances with the squirrels.

Daniel Nourozi (8)
Newark Hill Academy, Peterborough

When The Autumn Breeze Arrives

When the autumn breeze arrives,
The autumn leaves will dive,
Orange, brown and yellow fall from the trees,
The excited children jump in free.

Autumn is so beautiful,
Where everything is so colourful.
The birds hide from the cold breeze,
While squirrels snatch the acorns off the trees

Leaves are swirling, twirling,
Onto the ground,
Nuts are squashed, mashed,
Crushed into a mound.

Fatima Faisal (8)
Newark Hill Academy, Peterborough

Autumn Princess

Scarlet, brown conker waiting to be sent down a long tree.
Golden-brown leaves crunching step by step
Autumn sunlight and green grass with a hedgehog hiding in leaves.
Chestnut fire boiling hot, light brown, incredible!
Yellow, chestnut bird,
The bright light and green leaves.
The waterfall splashing and dashing.
The autumn princess twinkling and blinking.
Pretty flowers shining their prettiness everywhere.

Zainab Rafiq (8)
Newark Hill Academy, Peterborough

The Autumn Is Orange

Autumn is orange leaves twirling
Swaying in the air
Gliding down

The squirrels scurry to their home
Orange leaves fall to the ground
Kids jump into the piles of leaves

Squirrels get nuts
Then home to hide
Bears catch fish to eat

Autumn is chilled
Says whoosh when bored
Making a little tornado of leaves.

Joshua (8)
Newark Hill Academy, Peterborough

Autumn Painter

I can see the background and an autumn fairy with brown leaves and a shiny green dress, spinning around and spreading leaves.
The autumn leaves are falling on the ground,
Brown coffee light and crunchy leaves,
Chestnut leaves, yellow leaves,
Autumn horses and a shiny sun, autumn leaves on a tree.

Inaaya Ahmed (8)
Newark Hill Academy, Peterborough

Autumn Is Beautiful

Autumn is beautiful,
A cold breeze,
Squirrels snatching the acorns,
Off the trees.

Autumn is a princess
Making way for the breeze
Children jump in
As leaves come off the trees.

Khadijah Choudhury (8)
Newark Hill Academy, Peterborough

The Autumn Blowing

The autumn's a leaf blower
Happy and cheeky
Watch out behind you
Thiefy and sneaky

The autumn's a runner
Trying to catch leaves.
The big, orange leaves
Blowing around.

Sapphire Harrison (8)
Newark Hill Academy, Peterborough

Autumn Thief

Autumn thief can see pumpkins,
In the bad weather, he can hear leaves.
Crunching, he looks,
Grasping the chesnut trees.
Orange pumpkins he steals,
And hides them in his backpack.

Natas Maksimavicius (9)
Newark Hill Academy, Peterborough

Autumn

The autumn is chasing
Colourful leaves,
Like an acrobat
Swinging through the trees.

The conker king
Looking for his treasure,
Nuts lying on the floor,
Gold leaves flying at leisure.

Shia Mackereth Lopes (8)
Newark Hill Academy, Peterborough

Autumn

Autumn's a pirate
Stealing treasure
Snatching golden leaves
Rain started pouring
The autumn pirate ran away
In a huge ship
Colossus waves were hitting it.

Evan Puckys (8)
Newark Hill Academy, Peterborough

The Dull Dragon

The dragon's life was very full
With crimson scales soft as wool.
He did know why he was dull.
For breakfast, he ate a big seagull.
Then he said, "Ah, I see."
Someone shouted, "Help me!"
The dragon went with a dash,
A figure went fast as a flash.
The dragon said, "Ah, I see people don't like me."
"Maybe I can change things," I say.
The dragon said, "Hip hip hooray!"

Ezekiel Oyemakinde (9)
Sutton Oak CE Primary School, St Helens

My Magic Pencil Case

My magic pencil case has all sorts of stuff
Like rubbers, pens, pencils, even utensils!
I have stuff like... *bang!*
Wait, was that a bomb?
"Oh my gosh, why do you have to do that, Tom?"
Anyways, my magic pencil case has all sorts of stuff
Like burgers, hot dogs, even lollipops!
I have everything like...
"Argh, I ran out!"

Liana Mohammed (9)
Sutton Oak CE Primary School, St Helens

The GOAT

C ristiano is the best
R oyal as the royal family
I ncompetent as Mysterio himself
S uper as the mighty Zeus
T olerant to his fans
I ntelligent as Albert Einstein
A pproved as the best footballer
N ever gives up
O verpowered.

Emmanuel Olaojoyetan (9)
Sutton Oak CE Primary School, St Helens

Breakdancers Are Crazy

B e safe
R eally good
E xtremely fun
A tiring sport
K eep coming to be good
D ancers
A fun thing to do
N ever giving up
C orrection is key
E xtreme flares.

Harry Carruthers (9)
Sutton Oak CE Primary School, St Helens

Autumn For Good Luck

A utumn is very cold
U p in the sky, the leaves fly
T ree for good luck
U nregular leaves
M ud in the farms, mud in the grass
N eed to be warm, need to be cosy.

Lucia Graham (9)
Sutton Oak CE Primary School, St Helens

Summer

S ummer is the best season
U nder the shade, it's very cool
M y mum buys ice lollies
M ust go on the football pitch
E ngaged to summer
R ips my sweat out.

Jayden Lawrence (9)
Sutton Oak CE Primary School, St Helens

My Special Ham Sandwich

My ham sandwich is the best one yet.
My ham sandwich is the best to be.
My ham sandwich is better than my dad,
He just puts the whole packet on
But the only problem is it's my imagination!

Noah Gittins (9)
Sutton Oak CE Primary School, St Helens

Christmas Is Here

W inter is cold and freezing
I ce-cold like Antarctica
N ever miss the snow
T rees up for Christmas
E xtremely cold
R ed and green for Christmas.

Ianna Boslan (9)
Sutton Oak CE Primary School, St Helens

The Bald Eagle

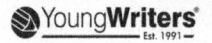

As the bald eagle with its wide wings
Flew through the sky searching for food
With its glowing amber eyes
It was getting hungry
So it grabbed a fish out of the water
And ate it.

Leighton Bamber (9)
Sutton Oak CE Primary School, St Helens

My Dog

I've got a dog, the cutest dog,
She's only one and is six feet long.
She's like a T-rex but they're extinct
So for now she is just my cute puppy dog.

Amelia Willis (10)
Sutton Oak CE Primary School, St Helens

Ronaldo

R unner
O pen net
N ow GOAT
A lways the GOAT
L ong shots
D irect freekick
O ver limits of football.

Charlie Jones (9)
Sutton Oak CE Primary School, St Helens

Christmas

I can see the cold ice snow.
I can hear the jingle bells.
I can taste the hot chocolate.
I can feel the heat of the fireplace.

Logan Pickering (10)
Sutton Oak CE Primary School, St Helens

Dance

D elightful
A mazing
N ice and pleasant
C omplicated for some
E xtra fun with fun.

Isobel Crawley (10)
Sutton Oak CE Primary School, St Helens

Winter Is Here

Cocoa milk
Jingle bells
Cosy season
Snow falling
Happy people
Present opening
Family meals.

Freddie Norton (9)
Sutton Oak CE Primary School, St Helens

We Need To Save The Ocean

We need to save the ocean.
We need to save the ocean.

As lightning strikes oceans surface,
He starts to fill with anger and sadness,
Crashing against the rugged rocks,
He protects the species like the sharks.

Within the morning sunlight glimmer,
The colourful corals wake from their slumber,
Whilst the waves stroke the sand carefully,
The dolphins dance and sing songs gracefully.

Ocean's coral welcome fish home,
No fish will be left alone,
All of the fish have their place in the system,
That is why we need their existence.

Ocean's tears run down his face,
Because he tastes a plastic taste,
As the corals turn ghostly white,
He cries and cries all through the night.

We need to save the ocean,
We need to save the ocean,
The ocean saves us.

Joe Williams (11)
The Meadows Primary Academy, Blurton

My Football Ran Away

"Mum! I'm going to play football with my friends."
Suddenly, my football! it's running away!
Outside down the streets as fast as the week started.
Popped into the field, dashed through a pile of dirt.
Ran a mile faster than Kyle, my friend.
Went on for weeks and days.
One day I spotted it again!
I was on the run,
It got faster and learned how to jump!
I got him cornered!
"Aha, I've got you! Huh, where is he?"
He jumped away.
"Get back here. Kyle, get that ball with me!"
My football vanished like a super secret spy.
Although all hope was lost for me,
We found him!
Popped back into my house, upstairs in my room,
Broke all my dirty plates.
And then... we got him
Back in my hand, anchored.
No more running away Mr Football.

Muhaiminul Karim Arish (10)
The Meadows Primary Academy, Blurton

A Delicate Door

One day I found myself in front of a delicate door,
I tried to walk away but I just couldn't ignore!
As I stepped in it was blacker than black,
However, it was too late to turn back!
My body started to feel strange,
I had a funny feeling in my brain,
Things began to become clear,
That my fancy family were no longer near.
As I began to see again,
I found a little gnome offering me some bread.
Not long later came a little cute bunny
Offering me some money.
Then in came Mum waking me from my fun.
I will never forgive her, I want payback.
Then she gave me a goody bag
With bread and money inside.
Then a teddy bunny and a teddy gnome appeared from behind,
What does this mean?
Could it all be true?

Annabelle Doyle (9)
The Meadows Primary Academy, Blurton

The Roller Coaster

I like to ride on roller coasters,
Up and down they go!
Here, there and everywhere,
I hope it's not too slow!

Up the lift hill, don't look down!
Holding on so tight,
Clank, clank, we're nearly there,
Squealing with delight!

Whoosh! Flying down we go,
My hands shoot up with glee,
My mum holds on, eyes closed so tight,
But this ride ain't scaring me!

Swirling, whirling, upside down,
My head spins round and round!
Way up high and back down low
And even underground!

The ride is slowing down now
And Mum is looking sick,
I help her off and lead the way,
"Let's go on the next ride quick!"

Ryder Smithson (8)
The Meadows Primary Academy, Blurton

Racing Rockets

We're going to have a race
In a very unique place.
It's very dark but it's full of stars
Where you see spaceships, never cars.
We're going to have a race
In a very unique place.
It's where ET tried to phone,
It's light-years away.
You might see asteroids on the way.
We're going to have a race
In a very unique place.
If you want to stay and never leave
You'll need a spacesuit to breathe.
We'll see the sun and the moon,
We'll end up at Neptune.
So fast you can't stop it,
There are no brakes on this rocket!
We're going to have a race
In a very unique place.

Jaydah Carter
The Meadows Primary Academy, Blurton

Animals And Pets

A nimals can be any colour like a rainbow
N ow they can be as big as a boulder
I n the jungle, they are as ferocious as an earthquake
M any animals live in different countries so there are lots of different noises
A ll animals are like humans a bit
L oud animals and pets are usually one kind and humans are all different
S ounds are very important for animals, like conversations are important to us

and

P ets are usually like most creatures
E very day they are there for you
T reat your pet like they are your human friend
S ounds are important for pets too.

Erin Underwood (10)
The Meadows Primary Academy, Blurton

Marcus Rashford

M arcus Rashford is an English footballer
A mazing he truly is
R ashford is my favourite football player
C areful when he has the ball
U sing himself as the weapon he protects the ball with all his might
S hooting is his speciality

R apid feet, eyes on goal
A tlanta Falcons don't stand a chance
S ay hi to the World Cup, Rashford
H appy days for him
F or him I give my heart
O n top of the football rank, you will find Rashford
R acing at the goal he will shoot, he will save
D ashing as a defender he will send the ball flying.

Phoebe Ann Coglon (9)
The Meadows Primary Academy, Blurton

Animals

Some animals live in the sea
And some live in the ocean.
Some animals live in a pond that is as big as a black hole or a little smaller.
Some fish live in fish shops so people can take them home for a pet.
A very big and dangerous animal is known as a shark.
There are different types of sharks like smile sharks, they always smile.
There are big animals like a whale.
There are animals that might be rare like axolotls.
There are animals that don't need saltwater like turtles.
Some turtles live on land, some live in the seawater
And some have regular water.

Harper Lear (9)
The Meadows Primary Academy, Blurton

Hey Let's Play A Video Game

Post a video on the internet of it just for fun!
Or maybe that's play for fun.
In the end, we will see who has won.
I really like Pokémon, also it's all about Mario.
The greatest character in Mario Kart is always going to be Mario!
I'd love to fight you
But maybe I'll let you pick the game or we could just draw sticks.
So here I've made a little cup filled with names of different games,
Just draw one popsicle stick and see which one of the names is on it.
That way we can make this easy
And can get back to our video games!

Lewis Harvey (9)
The Meadows Primary Academy, Blurton

The Riddle Of Time And Space

As big as a sun or bigger,
As black as space,
As mighty as the Roman army.
It could destroy anything,
It is big, it can explode if it gets too big,
The object is a black hole.

As small as the USA, white and real,
It was a make-belief planet,
It was once made by the Romans
And it is Pluto.

Shaped like a dome,
Carries extraterrestrials hunting for another planet,
This is a UFO.

It makes noise like an alien,
But is nothing like an alien,
It holds millions and millions of planets,
It is space itself.

Daniel Mair (9)
The Meadows Primary Academy, Blurton

Ghost Of The Mountains

Roar, roar, roar, I cannot roar,
I can purr, purr, meow, meow, hiss, hiss, growl and moan.

Fluffy, white and black, big paws,
Fear not snow showers.
Brahh, brahh, it's cold here,
However, I am well adapted to the cold environment.

Run, run, run,
I can run as fast as up to 40mph to catch my main prey,
The blue sheep, even though they are not blue.

Now you have read most of my poem
And are coming to the end,
I can now reveal that I am indeed the king of the snow,
The snow leopard.

James Day (8)
The Meadows Primary Academy, Blurton

Halloween

H alloween, as scary as a horror film
A fraid aliens trick or treating and eating sweets as they waddle around
L anterns lighting the whole street up with orange light
L arge crowds of children waiting to get their sour sweets
O range leaves on the floor swaying around
W alking along the street I see children in costumes
E ating sweets I see children knocking on doors
E njoying knocking on doors, I see children going home
N ot being scared I eat my sweet with hunger.

Amber Jones (9)
The Meadows Primary Academy, Blurton

Halloween

Happy Halloween is what they say,
But this Halloween shall make you afraid.
So let me tell you a story,
Not all children get lollipops and candy.
If you go trick or treating you may get a fright
Because the low-looking sun won't come to play,
So you get your treats but you can get tricks anywhere,
You may not get your wishes, it's usually candy you get
But wherever you go the night will follow you.
I wish you didn't but you do,
Even how hard you sleep or run there's always darkness.

Jovi Ray Smith (9)
The Meadows Primary Academy, Blurton

Gymnastics

G ymnastics is my favourite type of exercise
Y ay! And
M y mum takes me every week if I am good
N ow when I am playing with my friends we do it on the trampoline
A cross the house, I play gymnastics
S uper gymnastics always impresses me
T oday I did gymnastics, I loved it
I f I was in the Olympics doing gymnastics I would be so proud of myself
C arry on doing your best, you will soon be impressed
S oon you will get so good, trust me.

Miley Pattinson (8)
The Meadows Primary Academy, Blurton

The Environment Experience

E arth is our planet to enjoy our life
N ature is all around us
V ibrant, beautiful colours are everywhere
I n this world there is always some nature in front of us
R ecycle as much as you can to help the planet
O nly we can change it
N o Planet B
M agical moments are always brought to you
E scape to our favourite things in life
N ew adventures happen every day
T reat everybody how you would like to be treated.

Maddie Lamb (8)
The Meadows Primary Academy, Blurton

Fortnite And FC25

Item shop in Fortnite,
You get lots of cool skins.
Get V Bucks, skins and Emotes.
Play Battle Royale and mini games to get XP and level up
And you can get V Bucks from the Battle Pass.
Loads of fun to play with friends.
You can change skins at any time.
You can play with the best teams in football on FC25.
You can play with friends or with a team,
You can open packs and SBC.
You can play squad battles with friends,
You will love playing with friends.

George Mills (8)
The Meadows Primary Academy, Blurton

Nature

N ature is everywhere we go, woods, gardens and many more places around the world.
A ll flowers are beautiful, beautiful as can be, many are different and rare, so are we.
T ulips, a type and so are many more, so much more, flowers and countries too. All things are pretty just like
U s.
R ed cranesbill roses, daisies, also lots more like
E chinacea smells so nice like other flowers. Roses are red, violets are blue, smells so nice and so do you.

Layla Edwards (8)
The Meadows Primary Academy, Blurton

Space And Victory Over A Meteor

Space is amazing,
Amazing in different ways,
Always amazing,
Like how the Big Bang created our solar system
And how the moon came to orbit Earth.
Earth is our strength,
Earth is our life,
Gravity pulling us to the centre of our home planet,
Curiosity about aliens takes the lead,
Meteors moving towards us like a flash,
Crash!
Bang!
People screaming,
People panicking,
Peace has come
As we celebrate our victory.

Taylor-Bow Higginson (10)
The Meadows Primary Academy, Blurton

A Peculiar Door

As I lay there on the floor
I looked up and saw a peculiar door.
As I stood up and tried to walk back
I couldn't, it had all gone black.
When I woke up I gazed at fairies full of grace,
As I realised I wasn't meant to be in this place.
I ran and ran and ran until I came across a field full of green,
I sat on it and thought it was all just a dream.
I woke up and my dog led me to a piece of gloop
And I realised it was all just a loop.

Nicole Norcup (9)
The Meadows Primary Academy, Blurton

The Panda's Day Out

The little panda was sad
Because he did not have anyone to play with,
He opened the front door,
He went outside,
Slamming his feet on the grass
Until he found Mr Bear and Mr Dog.
He asked if he could play
And they said, "No."
So Panda was sad.
He went to his friend's house
And asked, "Do you want to play?"
They got him a surprise birthday party
And everyone was there
Even Mr Bear and Mr Dog.

Benjamin Harrison (9)
The Meadows Primary Academy, Blurton

Ancient Greeks

A phrodite, god of love and beauty
N ever afraid
C alm and trustworthy
I s always there to help others who need it
E ach god or goddess has their own power designated to them
N ever too rude to say hi
T he other gods and goddesses are called Zeus, Athena, Hermes, Hera, Ares, Artemis, Hades, Hephaestus, Poseidon, Demeter, Apollo, Dionysus and Hestia. All together there are fourteen Greek gods and goddesses.

Kaylee-Rae Gordon (10)
The Meadows Primary Academy, Blurton

Solar System

S illy Saturn spinning in the sky
O range and yellow is Venus
L ooking up in the air
A mazing Mercury as big as a skyscraper
R ed and orange is Mars

S un is as bright as a light
Y es, this is the solar system
S olar system is as purple as a magical door
T eal and green is the Earth that we live on
E ight planets in space
M ighty Neptune is grey and black.

Aubry-Lea Sketchley (9)
The Meadows Primary Academy, Blurton

Sad Animals

Each day I learn and read about the animals in need,
The circus rodeo, the fur and the factory farm,
The pain we cause them and the unbelievable harm!

The people who cause the pain
Chain them outside in snow or rain,
The innocent ones, they cannot raise their voice,
Let's raise our voices, let's keep a promise like I've kept mine,
It just takes effort and time!

Believe me, it takes effort and time!

Phoebe Green (8)
The Meadows Primary Academy, Blurton

A Sea Monster In My Pool!

There's a sea monster in my pool
And it won't go away.
There's a sea monster in my pool
And it won't obey
And I can't wait any longer for it to go away,
It won't leave me alone.
It could be my brother
But we'll never know anyway
And probably won't leave any day.
I found out it was my brother
But oh well, he's gone.
Anyway, I can finally enjoy a nice summer day in the pool.

Isabelle Burgess-Lowe (9)
The Meadows Primary Academy, Blurton

Friendship

F or your support and having fun with
R ight for telling secrets
I n and out when you need them
E ven if you fight you will never be apart
N ever break up as friends stick together forever
D oes never leave your side
S aves you from being bullied
H as your back and never leaves you
I s always there for help
P arties are fun with them when you have friendship.

Mya Davies (7)
The Meadows Primary Academy, Blurton

Plants Against Zombies

Plants are sprouting out,
There are dark and gloomy days,
Halloween comes, graveyards cursed,
Zombies coming to back gardens,
You plant a special seed,
A little plant comes out and starts shooting the zombies,
You find a new seed,
You plant the seed, a sunflower sprouts out,
It will heal your plants,
The zombies come back
The peashooters blast the zombies away
You get a new seed,
A cheeky bomb seed.

Thomas Hackney (11)
The Meadows Primary Academy, Blurton

Big Cats

You can hear a lion's roar from five miles away,
Tigers are very vicious species that look after their fierce family,
Jaguars climb trees like monkeys on vines,
A leopard doesn't change its spots,
Black panthers are leopards with a black coat,
A cheetah can run 65 to 75mph,
Snow leopards are well adapted to their cool environment,
White tigers are rare as there are only one in 10,000 left and are endangered.

Kye Comley (10)
The Meadows Primary Academy, Blurton

Tom Pidcock

Tom Pidcock comes in the inside line,
Overtakes his opponent.
Ten more laps to go in the XC Nationals
And Tom Pidcock is in first.
He's trying to win it for England and Britain.

Tom Pidcock is in the Olympics
And he is trying his hardest
To get in first but he's in second.
He takes the outside line
And gets in first.
He wins the Olympics for Great Britain.

Cameron Bowman (8)
The Meadows Primary Academy, Blurton

Superheroes

Batman, Flash and Spider-Man were at their homes,
But Iron Man was fighting The Joker.
He couldn't phone anyone because he wasn't playing around.
Then Iron Man died.
Flash heard Iron Man.
He went to fight and beat him.
Thirty minutes later, when Flash was going home he saw villains.
They were strong.
All the superheroes and villains were fighting.
The superheroes won.

Adrian Majkowski (8)
The Meadows Primary Academy, Blurton

The Crowd Of ST4!

Crowds chanting,
Crowds cheering,
People screaming,
Everyone goes wild,
Goal!

The players shout,
The fans jump up and down,
Stoke are 1-0 up,
It's the 90th minute,
They have a penalty,
To win the game,
To win the league.

Hearts beating,
Players crouched,
Bang!
Goal!
The trophy is going back to ST4!

Joseph Harrington (10)
The Meadows Primary Academy, Blurton

He's French

He can play left wing, right wing and striker,
He's like a Ninja Turtle,
He plays for Real Madrid
And his base card is 91 rated.

He's the GOAT,
He has three sons,
He plays for his national team
And played in Barcelona.

He's like a vampire,
He's a friend of Messi,
He played in the Copa America
And he played in Barcelona.

Charlie Cotterill (10)
The Meadows Primary Academy, Blurton

Football

F ootball is a sport where you use your feet
O n the pitch, I scored 77
O ctober is the best season in the world
T his is the best school ever
B righton is a football team that plays in a stadium
A ll the football teams are kind
L iverpool is the best football team in the world
L iverpool is also in our country.

Isaac Mellor (7)
The Meadows Primary Academy, Blurton

Uncanny Village

As the branches reached in front of our faces
We saw something glamorous.
What was it?
It was glistening in our eyes.
As we got closer it got brighter.
We entered the uncanny village...
We grabbed whatever was on the floor
And we ran for our lives,
A tribe was coming for us,
We heard chanting,
We made it home to see
What we picked up...

Lara Rauf (10)
The Meadows Primary Academy, Blurton

Animals

C uddly
A crobatic
T reats
S oftly purring.

D ogs like attention
O ther dogs run fast
G ood behaviour
S oftly purring.

H orses are nice
O n the grass and pavement horses can run
R is for radiant
S is for strength
E is for excellent.

Evelyn Pattinson (8)
The Meadows Primary Academy, Blurton

The Domain

Lions hung from claustrophobic canopies,
Trees stretched to the sky above,
Birdsong every second, every minute,
As rain ricocheted off the drenched floor,
As jaguars were prepared to pounce,
Vultures hung high
And yet we still explore the wonder lands,
The ecosystem,
Our home,
The world,
Get ready to get your mind blown
By nature.

Yusuf Aiybokhaodu
The Meadows Primary Academy, Blurton

Kirby And The Dimensional Portal

In a far, far away galaxy, there was a star called Planet Popstar
And there was a pink blob called Kirby.

Once he was eating cake but a dimensional portal appeared!
It led to a PS5 where the robotic hero is and his name is Astro!

An island, where materials live, Cuphead, Cuphead is his name!
Kirby went through a lot but this was the craziest!

Davi Silveira Cozzo Tajariol (8)
The Meadows Primary Academy, Blurton

All About Friendship!

Friendship is really important,
You can have fun all the time.
Real friends are fun,
When you have fun you forget about your worries.
It's always fun to have friends because they never let you give up.
You can always have fun without your family when you're with your friends.
This was all about friendship!
You can have fun with friends.

Isla Cooper (8)
The Meadows Primary Academy, Blurton

Halloween

H alloween is joyful for all of us
A day that makes everyone happy
L ove the candy and all
L ike the spooky moves
O nly wear wonderful spooky clothes
W atch the spooky decorations
E njoy the tricks and sweets
E verything is really exciting
N othing is absolutely boring.

Jagoda (7)
The Meadows Primary Academy, Blurton

The Meadows

M agnificent meadows ready to learn
E nthusiastic pupils excited to learn
A cademic students listening to teachers
D ifferent backgrounds, respected by seniors
O thers like different schools but this is my best
W onderful peers respect the values
S afe, smart students never get confused.

Vincent Ehimen (10)
The Meadows Primary Academy, Blurton

Seasons

S easons are part of the world
E very single one tells its own story
A utumn is when leaves turn red and gold
S ummer is scorching hot, a beach is for summer
O thers like winter make your lips turn to ice
N ow there is one left to tell you about
S pring is when flowers fill the grass.

Evan Robotham (10)
The Meadows Primary Academy, Blurton

A Dragon In My Wardrobe

There's a dragon in my wardrobe
But maybe that's just my sister,
As fierce as a mythical animal,
As feisty as a tiger's paw,
Aiming for trouble and lots more bubbles.
Getting mum on her side, getting dad on her side,
I hope I live but that is not for certain,
Wish me luck, if I even get time for enough.

Edom Aregay (9)
The Meadows Primary Academy, Blurton

About Me

I 'm Imogen Speake,
M y favourite food is chicken noodles,
O nly when it is snowing a lot I build snowmen with my brother,
G oing on a car ride to my nan's is fun because she lives far,
E very time I see my dog called Narla I smile,
N ever will I not help my amazing friends.

Imogen Speake (9)
The Meadows Primary Academy, Blurton

Young Bear Cub

Beside you young bear cub, your beloved mother passing by.
Above you young bear cub, doves flying by.
Around you young bear cub, butterflies asking why?
Along the stream young bear cub, otters feeling shy.
Upon a Lily, Bees looking up at the big blue sky.
Everywhere you look a graceful sprout of nature loves life.

Aimee Flynn (10)
The Meadows Primary Academy, Blurton

All About Puppies

Playing with puppies is fun
Because they are kind.

Up and down with a puppy,
You will have entertainment.

People love puppies.

People need to play with puppies
Because they always want to play.

You always need to stay aware Chihuahuas can hurt you
But some are kind.

Samuel Cragg (7)
The Meadows Primary Academy, Blurton

Football

F ill the stadium
O n the pitch players score
O n the grass, they run as fast as a cheetah
T ime to take a break
B ang, a ball crashes into the net
A ll the fans go wild
L ike a lion, the fans scream
L ike a bird, the ball flew in the air.

Lottie Colclough (10)
The Meadows Primary Academy, Blurton

My Culture

C ome and join us to see what my culture is like
U nlike here in England, it's warm all around
L ike Trinidad, it still rains
T rinidad and Tobago is where I originate from
U nlike London, our carnival was made first
R espect our culture
E njoy this poem.

Caleb Almarales (10)
The Meadows Primary Academy, Blurton

Space Is Amazing

Space is amazing,
There are planets,
There are stars,
There's the moon,
There's the sun,
It may be dark, but it always is,
Meteors shoot down like lightning,
Stars are small,
Stars shine bright,
Stars are always in the sky,
Even when it's light
Space is amazing.

Amber Clowes (10)
The Meadows Primary Academy, Blurton

Marvel

M ighty heroes, untied they stand,
A mazing powers in the world so grand.
R eady to fight for justice and right,
V ictory shines in epic fights.
E ndless stories of courage unfold,
L egends of Marvel be awesome and the best and don't forget Marvel can beat anyone.

Shahzaib Akhtar (8)
The Meadows Primary Academy, Blurton

Witches

W itches make mysterious potions
I n the sky, they soar
"T o the sky," they say to their brooms
C ats are their magical companions
H er cat will creep up on you
"E eek," someone screams
"S ave me," the people who see them say.

Harlow Gollins (9)
The Meadows Primary Academy, Blurton

Lamborghini

L amborghini as fast as lightning,
A s cool as ice,
M adness in real life,
B ig engine
O riginal car
R enowned all over the world
G ot so much speed
H yper car
I ncredible car
N ice and fast
I ncredible car.

Harley Lear (10)
The Meadows Primary Academy, Blurton

Run Rabbit Run!

Run rabbit run
All you can you've escaped for now.
Run rabbit run
But not for long, I will find you.
Run rabbit run
Or I will find a new prey and trap.
Run rabbit run
You might have known them but unless they're smart like you they will stay and be my friend!
Run rabbit run!

Ivy Turner (8)
The Meadows Primary Academy, Blurton

Animals You See In The Seasons

In summer I always see birds dancing with glee,
In spring I always see ducks testing their luck,
In autumn I always see squirrels feasting on their nuts,
In winter I hear animals in their nests,
In all the seasons, I see a variety of animals
But most importantly I have fun looking at them all.

Lola Wakelin (10)
The Meadows Primary Academy, Blurton

Autumn Is Coming

A mazing trees
U nderneath piles of leaves, hedgehogs live
T he leaves are falling down
U nder the trees, families have picnics
M um says it's too cold to go and play
N ature is starting to hibernate.

Well, I guess it's time for autumn.

Evie Salmon (9)
The Meadows Primary Academy, Blurton

Summertime

S un shines on the blossoming flowers
U nder the warmth of the sun children play
M any trees bloom new leaves and waving branches
M any motionless people have a break
E aster still hides in the flourishing flowers
R elaxing parents tan in the burning sun.

Lily Sutton (10)
The Meadows Primary Academy, Blurton

Friendship

A friend is there for you no matter what,
They are there for all your ups and downs.
A friend is with you forever,
They love you forever.
They will never judge you.
True friends are close, never far.
They will always be honest.
They are hard to find
So treasure them forever.

Olivia-Rae Nicklin (10)
The Meadows Primary Academy, Blurton

Football

F ootball is my favourite sport
O n the pitch, I'm good at goalkeeping
O n the pitch, I'm good at defending
T otal emotion
B e kind on the pitch
A t football, I'm good and calm
L ove the game
L eave it all on the pitch.

Cody Prince (10)
The Meadows Primary Academy, Blurton

Football Champion

R ashford relies on himself and plays good
A n amazing applauding player
S o above average and fantastic
H appy, cheerful player
F riendly, reliable footballer
O n pitch player
R isky and reliable
D ainty, daydreaming player.

Eleesie Lily Thorley
The Meadows Primary Academy, Blurton

Dancing

D ance is the best
A t night the light on the wall is cool
N ight at quarter to seven
C an they change the time? Everybody says good afternoon
I n the room it's cool
N ow we get on the dance floor
G o do the dance with the helpers.

Tilly-Mae Podmore (7)
The Meadows Primary Academy, Blurton

Football

He scores magnificent goals
He is a striker
He plays for Stoke
He is on a pirate ship
His base card is 71.
Who is he?

He is very skilful
He is fast
He is short
He played for PSG
He is at Inter Miami
And his base card is 95.
Who is he?

Jacob Dillon (10)
The Meadows Primary Academy, Blurton

Racing

R acing lightning fast like a speedy race car
A s fast as an engine thumping in a truck
C ruising down the M6 going at lightning speed
I n the light, you can take a glimpse
N o one will take over this beast
G o as fast as the motorway.

Harley Carr (8)
The Meadows Primary Academy, Blurton

Ronaldo

Fans were surrounding the pitch
Because all the Ronaldo fans love Ronaldo.
Once Ronaldo did a very crazy trick
When he was practising with his team.
One time Ronaldo was playing a match,
Then he scored a goal so his mates hugged him.
He was playing on a cool pitch.

Reggie Rowland (7)
The Meadows Primary Academy, Blurton

The Jungle

Jaguars creep up on the jungle floor,
Waiting for their chance to strike.

Underneath the canopy lies a hidden world,
With adventures waiting for anyone and everyone.

Night rises upon the jungle as the jungle's animals
Hide in the impenetrable foliage.

Noah Lovatt (11)
The Meadows Primary Academy, Blurton

Winter

W hen it's snowing,
 I t's time to build a snowman,
N ow when it's raining,
T he snow thaws away.
E njoy the seasons as we play with the snow,
R elaxing, watching Christmas films while the children are catching snowflakes.

Tia Shey (9)
The Meadows Primary Academy, Blurton

Fairies

F antastic, beautiful fairies are my favourite
A mazing fairies have wands that sparkle in the light
I maginative fairies love Mother Nature
R are fairies can be seen in the magical forest
Y oung little girls if you see a fairy believe in them.

Isabelle Moran-Bamford (9)
The Meadows Primary Academy, Blurton

What Am I?

Looking out the window to darkness as dark as night,
Eating special foods and drinking from special containers,
Need to keep one eye open to see where we are going,
We are living in a light space with lots of equipment.
What am I?
I am an astronaut in space!

Noah Smith-Harrison (9)
The Meadows Primary Academy, Blurton

A Sky Of Wonders

Running through the meadows of flowers,
Feeling the tulips on my fingertips,
As I look into the sky I wonder,
I wonder what lies above the clouds,
I wonder if there is a world of birds,
I wonder if there is a world of shining stars,
I wonder, I wonder.

Lyla Ridge (10)
The Meadows Primary Academy, Blurton

Football Riddles

He is a striker,
He plays for Real Madrid,
He played in the Euros,
He used to play for PSG,
He is Mbappé.

I play for FC Barcelona,
I played in the Euros,
I won the Euros,
I am a wonder kid in Spain,
I am Lamine Yamal.

Callum Ford (10)
The Meadows Primary Academy, Blurton

Fantasy Land!

Fairies fly like butterflies in the sky,
Mystical plants flourish over,
Fluffy clouds watch above,
Where rainbows arch
And the unicorns gallop,
Enchanted forests
With fire-breathing dragons,
In this fantasy land,
In this fantasy land.

Ivy Clarke (10)
The Meadows Primary Academy, Blurton

Thor

The Greek gods are gory,
Thor, the god of thunder,
He roars in rage when he is no longer happy,
He can cause earthquakes, tsunamis and volcanic eruptions,
So you best not get on his bad side or you'll be in trouble.
Trust me, I'm not lying.

Thomas Fairbanks (9)
The Meadows Primary Academy, Blurton

Halloween

H alloween is spooky
A time to dress up
L anterns shining
L ollipops collecting
O utside knocking on everyone's doors
W icked witch
E vil vampire
E yeball
N aughty or nice.

Tia Hilton (10)
The Meadows Primary Academy, Blurton

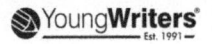

What Is It?

Large as elephants,
Strong as tigers,
Dangerous as a T-rex,
Hundreds are in the world that exist,
It has red flaming eyes,
It can fly wherever it wants,
It can destroy villages,
It can be red or other colours.
It's a dragon!

Ibrahim Mahammad (8)
The Meadows Primary Academy, Blurton

Animals

Beetles scurrying
Lambs jumping
Meerkats standing
Lions roaring
Butterflies flying
Foxes running
Dogs barking
Cats purring
Snakes hissing
Wolves howling
Giraffes as tall as trees
Cheetahs as fast as wild hippos.

Destiny Babic (9)
The Meadows Primary Academy, Blurton

Mbappé

M bappé is a 2018 World Cup champion
B est Real Madrid player in 2024/2025
A s fast as a racing car
P layer is a French superstar
P layer is a striker
É very French fan likes Mbappé.

Amadou Mbengue (8)
The Meadows Primary Academy, Blurton

Planets

Mysteries above the atmosphere,
Stars shine bright like diamonds,
Planets orbit the sun,
Galaxies swarm the planets,
Planets, blue, red and orange too,
Some have rings and some don't,
Planets shine whilst soaring through the air.

Isla-Rose Summerhayes (10)
The Meadows Primary Academy, Blurton

Eagles

E agles soaring through the sky
A lways chasing their prey
G reatest type of bird
L emon doves don't stand a chance
E agle's eggs always safe
S pecial types of eagles like golden or bald eagles.

Freddie Cragg (9)
The Meadows Primary Academy, Blurton

Friendship

Friends are really important to me
Because they are like family.
If you think about it,
Two people called Adam and Eve are basically our parents
Because they were the first people alive,
Make sure you find true people to be your friends.

Michael Giblin (10)
The Meadows Primary Academy, Blurton

The Witch

Today, I'm going camping,
A noise called me to it.
Behind the trees was a witch,
I started running as she chased me.
"I want you for dinner."
The witch was very annoyed.
After dinner she was nice.
What a mystery.

Amelia Allt (9)
The Meadows Primary Academy, Blurton

Football

F ootball is fun
O verhead kick
O i, come and join my team
T ime to score lots of goals
B eat every team in football
A sk lots of questions
L eft-footed
L eant referee money.

Sebastian Mellor (9)
The Meadows Primary Academy, Blurton

Autumn

We have hot chocolate in our house.
We decorate.
It is so much fun.
The monsters come out.
We go trick or treating.
So much fun.
Many decorations.
We get lots of sweets.
It is Halloween.
Have a good Halloween.

Eivelyn Baldwin (8)
The Meadows Primary Academy, Blurton

Autumn

A utumn is my favourite month
U nder my feet, autumn leaves crunch and munch.
T oday autumn comes
U nderneath the bright yellow sun,
M isty morning come,
N ight sky as dark as bats' wings.

Daisy Preston (9)
The Meadows Primary Academy, Blurton

Snow, Snow, Snow

Snow twirls and swirls
From the glittering sky
Covering the ground
Like a fluffy blanket
Boys and girls scream in excitement
And begin to run around grabbing snow
And having fun playing with their friends all day long.

Harrison Crayton (7)
The Meadows Primary Academy, Blurton

Solar System

S entimental Saturn and its beautiful rings
P luto is tiny but mighty
A stronomical wonders fill the darkness
C louds of dusty darkness roam around
E xtraterrestrial creatures rule outer space.

Charlie Kean (9)
The Meadows Primary Academy, Blurton

Dragon In My Basement

D ad checking in my basement
R oaring as loud as a fierce dinosaur and dad screaming
A iming for me
G randad getting galloped
O n the basement floor dragon eating away
N ot my day.

Ezaan Raza (9)
The Meadows Primary Academy, Blurton

Space

Out of this world, there was a man called Neil Armstrong
Who was the first person to walk on the moon.

Galaxy Swirl in green and blues,
Our sun blazes brilliant orange.

Darkest black of endless space.

Ryley Seadon (9)
The Meadows Primary Academy, Blurton

Friends Forever – Never Leave Me!

We watch movies with popcorn together.
We care about other people.
We play together all the time.
We are besties forever.
We help our friends.
We stick to our friend's side.
We are BFFs forever.

Jessica Cliffe (7)
The Meadows Primary Academy, Blurton

My Football Debut

F ierce rivalries
O n the pitch of glory
O n the wall of fame
T he winning goal
B eautiful game
A live winner
L iving champion
L ive to win.

Ralph Clarke (8)
The Meadows Primary Academy, Blurton

Halloween Night

Leaves falling off the trees.
Decorations swinging in the wind.
Pumpkins lit in the windows.
Children screaming and laughing out loud.
The moon shines bright.
Trick or treat?
Lots of sweets.

Peyton Harnett (8)
The Meadows Primary Academy, Blurton

The Sun

A kennings poem

Skin burner
Sky lighter
As bright as plasma
Cloud clearer
Moon shiner
Ice melter
Fire bringer
Planet puller
Heat producer
Light bringer
Life giver
Energy releaser.

Dacey Jones (9)
The Meadows Primary Academy, Blurton

Space

What am I?
I am high in the sky.
I shimmer like a star which is as bright as the sun.
I am Saturn.

What am I?
I am dark and light.
I may look small but I am big.
I am the moon.

Klayton Mellor (10) & Jessica Ann Pass (9)
The Meadows Primary Academy, Blurton

Horses

H appy trotting hooves
O n open fields, we race
R iding through the countryside
S addle upon our backs
E ating hay and apples
S peeding away when we gallop.

Lexie Concliffe (10)
The Meadows Primary Academy, Blurton

Football Is Amazing

F lip around
O verhead kicks
O kay, I am awesome
T ricks are my speciality
B rave
A nd strong
L ively and fun
L ove football forever.

Oscar Edge (8)
The Meadows Primary Academy, Blurton

Unicorn

Unicorns are cute
And they have rainbow hair.
They are never mean to people
And they live in the air.
They eat candy for dinner every day
Or they can eat a rainbow popcorn breakfast as well.

Ava Emami (8)
The Meadows Primary Academy, Blurton

The Rainbow

Despite the storm what will it be?
A bird, a plane, a buzzing bee?
Despite the storm what will it be?
And at last, it's free!
Along the sun, the rain,
There it is, it's a rainbow.

Emil Joby (9)
The Meadows Primary Academy, Blurton

Weather

Rain and thunder hammering down,
Worms crawling out of the ground.
Suddenly, the sun comes out,
The worms retreat under the ground.
Calm and peaceful at last,
Today is a very good day.

Jack Sellers (9)
The Meadows Primary Academy, Blurton

Hop, Hop, Hop Bunny

B unnies hop, hop, hop
U nder the ground they live
N ever mind the scary boy in the window
N ever say his name out loud or he will kill you
Y ou will be next.

Gracie Oates (9)
The Meadows Primary Academy, Blurton

Space

S pace has low gravity
P eace and quiet up in the air
A stronauts in their rocket
C oming to space with friends
E agle-like people flying in every direction.

Muhammad Narooz (9)
The Meadows Primary Academy, Blurton

What Is It?

It's as sharp as a needle.
It's as cute as a teddy bear.
It sleeps through the cold.
It's as loved as a house cat.
It's endangered like a panda.
It's a hedgehog!

Penelope Woodall (10)
The Meadows Primary Academy, Blurton

Dance

Dance is a magical place to be
Where wonder comes,
You're learning new dances every step of the way,
Going to competitions, coming first place,
Making new friends, hip hip hooray.

Eliza-Rae Steveson (10)
The Meadows Primary Academy, Blurton

Space!

S tars twinkling like little lights
P lanets spinning slowly
A liens bouncing higher than cats
C omets zooming and shining
E arth is everyone's home.

Marnie Cartlidge (8)
The Meadows Primary Academy, Blurton

Freddie

F ootball is my hobby
R eady to kick off
E at my breakfast
D rive to the pitch
D rink water
I am a LB
E uro 2034 here I come.

Freddie Hughes (8)
The Meadows Primary Academy, Blurton

Messi

M essi has amazing skills
E very time he has the ball he scores
S o he wears the number 10
S o he has lots of trophies
I know he has lots of money.

Harrison Crayton (7)
The Meadows Primary Academy, Blurton

Sloths

S loths are my favourite
L ots of love for them
O thers find them cuddly
T hey are just so cute
H e is my friend
S o I love them.

Eden Rose (8)
The Meadows Primary Academy, Blurton

A Secret Lion

A thumping beast who is roaring,
The king of the jungle,
Making up a fight.
One of the strong cats,
Nature's bravest creature,
A thumping beast who is roaring.

Aylan Rhys Lapi (8)
The Meadows Primary Academy, Blurton

Guess The Character

She is a vegetarian.
She likes blue.
She makes thousands of songs.
She goes on the stage.
She has lots of fans.
She is a famous singer.
She is Taylor Swift.

Jessica Gilham (7)
The Meadows Primary Academy, Blurton

Zeus

Z eus is the god of thunder
E gyptians were long before
U se your goodness to stop his anger
S ometimes if he gets too mad he will strike thunder.

Harper Howell (9)
The Meadows Primary Academy, Blurton

Football

People cheering,
Shouting loudly,
Football players scoring,
Taking penalties,
Footballers scoring goals,
Fans cheering in the distance,
It's football.

Freddie Ridge (7)
The Meadows Primary Academy, Blurton

Games

G ames are my favourite thing to play
A ny game, any day
M aybe I will play a new game
E verything is fun
S o let's have some fun.

Joshua Millard (8)
The Meadows Primary Academy, Blurton

Football

F uture
O n the pitch
O n the net
T ake a shot
B all
A fan loves football
L oud fans
L ose or win.

Ada Watts (8)
The Meadows Primary Academy, Blurton

Eyes Shiny Like...

Eyes blue like the sky.
Eyes clear as diamonds.
Eyes tranquil like water.
Eyes green like emeralds.
Eyes bright like the moon.
Eyes as shiny as the stars.

John Osei (10)
The Meadows Primary Academy, Blurton

School

S weet loads of smiles
C ool, cheerful
H onest and healthy
O verjoyed, original
O utstanding
L earn and be loving!

Sharon Gwandu (9)
The Meadows Primary Academy, Blurton

What Is It?

It has wings as big as a bean.
It doesn't exist.
It's scaly.
It's powerful.
It has four legs.
It has sharp teeth.
It's a dragon.

Oliver Loftus (7)
The Meadows Primary Academy, Blurton

Lionel Messi

He's in Argentina,
He plays for Inter Miami,
He's one of the best,
Football players in the world.
He's number 10.
He's Lionel Messi.

Dominik Olah (7)
The Meadows Primary Academy, Blurton

Guess It!

It is bigger than a flower.
It is white with some black.
It is a sphere with no sides.
It can be called two things.
It's a football or a soccer ball.

Aronas Avdulovas (8)
The Meadows Primary Academy, Blurton

The Dead Place

A murder of crows flying in circles,
Surrounding a dead deer.
Hunters looking for food for their family.
Trees reaching the roaring thunderclouds.

Ideraoluwa Aliu (10)
The Meadows Primary Academy, Blurton

Butterfly

Butterflies flap their wings.
They make the world look beautiful.
Best friends with flowers.
Love the yellow pollen.
Make the world better.

Charlotte White (7)
The Meadows Primary Academy, Blurton

Space

S tars gleaming
P lanets swirling
A stronauts watching
C olours spreading
E xtraterrestrials living.

Siena Cooper (11)
The Meadows Primary Academy, Blurton

Gorilla

Fierce and muscular
King of the jungle
Brave and mighty
Energetic and playful
Mysterious and stunning
Boisterous and sneaky.

Ethan Cope (8)
The Meadows Primary Academy, Blurton

Who Is She?

She has green and black hair.
She has a green top and shorts.
She has lots of concerts.
She sings.
She's Billie Eilish.

Charlotte Dawson (8)
The Meadows Primary Academy, Blurton

Swimming In A Refreshing Pool

Diving in, yay, yay.
Going to competitions, coming second place.
Learning new skills every day.
That is just my game, yay, yay.

Nyla Bosha (11)
The Meadows Primary Academy, Blurton

Sonic

S uper fast
O nly after the rings
N ever gives up
I n my favourite game
C ollects emeralds.

Wilfred Lees (7)
The Meadows Primary Academy, Blurton

World Cup

Best footballer
Very rich
Lots of World Cups
Plays video games
He has lots of golden footballs
He's Messi!

Alan Joby (7)
The Meadows Primary Academy, Blurton

Cat On The Mat

A beautiful cat on a blue mat.
A cute cat on a big mat.
A silly cat on a patterned mat.
A lovely cat on a wonderful mat.

Victoria Ptak (8)
The Meadows Primary Academy, Blurton

Friends

Friends are forever,
They are really kind to people.
I am a good friend,
I share with everyone,
I respect people.

Avia Helliwell (7)
The Meadows Primary Academy, Blurton

Magic

M agnificent magic
A ncient magic
G oofy magic
I ncredible magic
C reepy magic.

Olivia Coglon
The Meadows Primary Academy, Blurton

Pet

It's fluffy.
It's cute.
It's annoying.
It chases light.
I love it.
It's my dog, Vinnie!

Roman Adams (7)
The Meadows Primary Academy, Blurton

Cats

C ute, cuddly cats
A dorable, awesome, amazing
T ill they no longer last
S ad, sad, sad.

Safoorah Malik (9)
The Meadows Primary Academy, Blurton

Spider-Man

A kennings poem

Web slinger
Crime fighter
City protector
Mary-Jane lover
Identity protector.

Harley Brian (10)
The Meadows Primary Academy, Blurton

Dragon's Catch

A dragon flew by,
He saw a guy,
He stared at him,
The guy's name is Jim.

Maximilian Almarales (8)
The Meadows Primary Academy, Blurton

Unicorns

Unicorns are pretty,
They are soft and cute,
They can fly,
I love unicorns.

Ellie Cole-Pye (7)
The Meadows Primary Academy, Blurton

Reading

Reading a book is fun
I need lots of books
Relax at home
Finish the pages.

Emma Jandzikova (8)
The Meadows Primary Academy, Blurton

The Moon

People look at the moon
It is bright
It is shiny
And there are aliens.

Isaac Nicklin (7)
The Meadows Primary Academy, Blurton

Unicorn

Unicorns fly
In the sky
And leave
Sparkles and presents.

Charlee-May O'Brien (7)
The Meadows Primary Academy, Blurton

YOUNG WRITERS INFORMATION

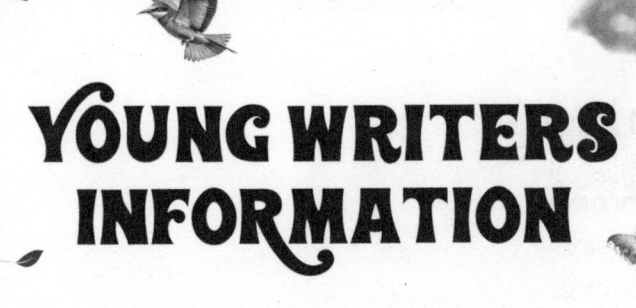

We hope you have enjoyed reading this book – and that you will continue to in the coming years.

If you're the parent or family member of an enthusiastic poet or story writer, do visit our website **www.youngwriters.co.uk/subscribe** and sign up to receive news, competitions, writing challenges and tips, activities and much, much more! There's lots to keep budding writers motivated!

If you would like to order further copies of this book, or any of our other titles, then please give us a call or order via your online account.

Young Writers
Remus House
Coltsfoot Drive
Peterborough
PE2 9BF
(01733) 890066
info@youngwriters.co.uk

Join in the conversation!
Tips, news, giveaways and much more!

 YoungWritersUK   YoungWritersCW

 youngwriterscw   youngwriterscw